You'll Always Be My Baby

Copyright © 2006 by Sara Evans, Tony Martin, Tom Shapiro

Published in Nashville, Tennessee, by Thomas Nelson. Thomas Nelson is a trademark of Thomas Nelson, Inc.

Project Editor: Lisa Stilwell

Photo on page 60 and the back cover taken by Russ Harrington, Nashville, TN   www.russharrington.com

Photo on page 61 taken by Robert Ascroft

Design by Juicebox Designs, Nashville, Tennessee www.juiceboxdesigns.com
Hand Lettering by Kerri Charlton

ISBN-10: 1-4041-0451-8
ISBN-13: 978-1-4041-0451-8

Printed and bound in the United States

www.thomasnelson.com

SARA EVANS

with Tony Martin & Tom Shapiro

COUNTRYMAN

You'll Always Be My Baby

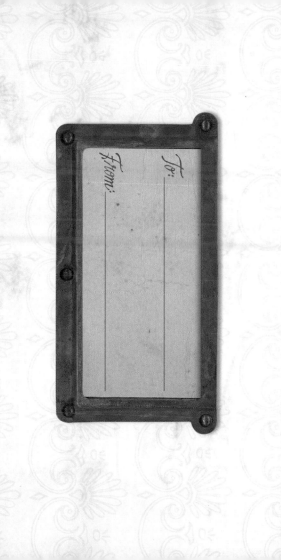

To:

From:

Unconditional love: It's unwavering, steadfast, selfless, and forgiving. I didn't truly understand this until I became a parent. With the birth of each of my three children, my understanding has grown exponentially.

"You'll Always Be My Baby" is an anthem of unconditional love. When Tony, Tom, and I wrote this song, our goal was to convey just how important it is in our own lives to give and receive true love. God loves us unconditionally and He asks us to share that love with one another. This is not always an easy task, but when we do choose to offer or accept unconditional love, it is very empowering!

We are faced with many choices in life. Sometimes, unfortunately, we or our loved ones make the wrong decisions. But the power of love and forgiveness can restore and redeem. With this song and this book, I am hopeful we all will pause and reflect on the beauty of life, of love, and of each other.

Sara

There I was

Ten Years old

waiting

in my room for him

to come home

EVERY EVERY THERE'S A TUG TO CHOOSE BETWEEN RIGHT

DAY

MINUTE

OF WAR

AND WRONG

And I just knew

He'd be so mad

Though I begged

my mother not to,

she told my dad

There was I had let

no denying burying him down

WE'VE ALL BEEN THERE . . . .

It's time to face the consequences

And the waiting is so hard

Your imagination runs wild

Your throat gets tight

It's hard to breathe

Oh, if only you could go back in time,

And do things differently.

But instead of being angry

he put his arms

around me and said

In the sunlight and the rain

Brightest nights or darkest days

I'll always

feel the same way

SHOW LOVE

and watch it

MEND

REPAIR

HEAL

MANIFEST

Whatever road you may be on

Know you're never too far gone

My love is there

wherever you may be

Just remember that
you'll always be
my baby

There was
I had let

MATTERS

MOMENT

SO RIGHT . . .

ANYTHING BE WRONG?

ANOTHER DAY

GOING BACK

DON'T LOVE YOURSELF?

no denying

God down

upon

But instead of being angry

He let His love surround

me and I heard

In the sunlight and the rain

Brightest nights or

darkest days

I'll always

feel the same way

DON'T YOU KNOW

Whether you're high above the sky

or in the deepest ocean

nothing in all creation can separate My love from you . . .

You are forgiven

You have My promise

Yesterday

Today

Tomorrow

Whatever road you may be on

Know you're never too far gone

My love is there —

wherever you may be

Just remember that
you'll always be
my baby

MY LOVE IS THERE

Walking

alone

Driving

too fast

Running

from life

Crawling

to a place of rest . . .

There he is

my little man

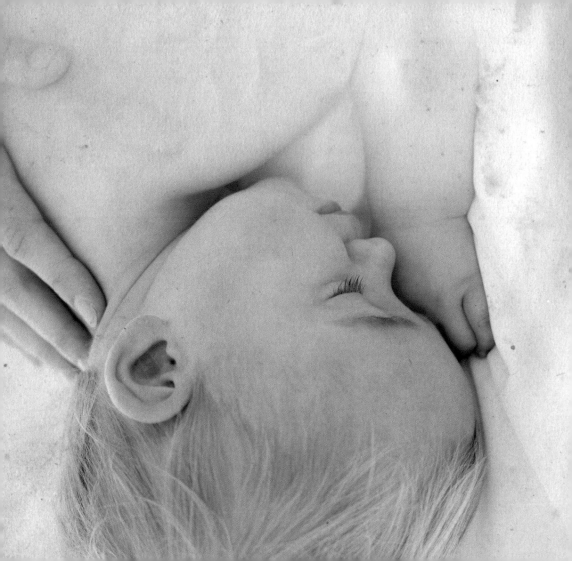

NEW LIFE

Love revealed

Fearfully and wonderfully made

Meant to be

Perfect

Loved beyond the hemisphere

I'm sure he'll get in trouble
every now and then

And I pray to God

That when he does

I'll be just as understanding

as my father was

IT'S YOUR TURN

to remember

and continue the course

love put you on

'Cause the last thing I is let him down

So instead of being angry

I'm gonna throw my arms around

him and I'll say

In the sunlight or the rain

Brightest nights or darkest days

I'll always feel the same way

wanna do

CHOOSE TODAY

IT'S THE RIGHT
TO PAVE THE WAY

FOR LOVE TO

LOVE

AND TOMORROW
AND THE NEXT DAY

CHOICE

CONTINUE

Whatever road you may be on

Know you're never too far gone

My love is there

wherever you may be

Just remember that you'll always be my baby

SOW LOVE

REAP LOVE

Pass it on

Continue the circle

Be a strand in the chord of love that binds

Hold together

BY LOVE PASSED DOWN

You'll Always Be

There I was —
Ten years old
Waiting in my room for him to
come home
And I just knew
He'd be so mad
Though I begged my mother not
to, she told my dad
There was no denying I had let
him down
But instead of being angry
he put his arms around me
and said

In the sunlight or the rain
Brightest nights or darkest days
I'll always feel the same way
Whatever road you may be on
Know you're never too far gone
My love is there wherever you
may be
Just remember that
you'll always be my baby

My Baby

There I was
Twenty-one
I was so ashamed of what I'd done
On a country road
Parked one night
What started out so innocent
crossed the line
There was no denying I had let
God down
But instead of being angry, He let
His love surround me
and I heard

In the sunlight or the rain
Brightest nights or darkest days
I'll always feel the same way
Whatever road you may be on
Know you're never too far gone
My love is there wherever you
may be
Just remember that
you'll always be my baby

There he is
My little man
I'm sure he'll get in trouble every
now and then
And I pray to God
That when he does
I'll be just as understanding as my
father was
'Cause the last thing I wanna do is
let him down
So instead of being angry I'm gonna
throw
my arms around him and I'll say

In the sunlight or the rain
Brightest nights or darkest days
I'll always feel the same way
Whatever road you may be on
Know you're never too far gone
My love is there wherever you
may be
Just remember that
you'll always be my baby